THE CONSPIRACY OF YOU

LAKESHA MATHIS

BALBOA.
PRESS

A DIVISION OF HAY HOUSE

Balboa Press books may be ordered through booksellers or by contacting:

Balboa Press
A Division of Hay House
1663 Liberty Drive
Bloomington, IN 47403
www.balboapress.com
1 (877) 407-4847

Because of the dynamic nature of the Internet, any web addresses or links contained in this book may have changed since publication and may no longer be valid. The views expressed in this work are solely those of the author and do not necessarily reflect the views of the publisher, and the publisher hereby disclaims any responsibility for them.

The author of this book does not dispense medical advice or prescribe the use of any technique as a form of treatment for physical, emotional, or medical problems without the advice of a physician, either directly or indirectly. The intent of the author is only to offer information of a general nature to help you in your quest for emotional and spiritual well-being. In the event you use any of the information in this book for yourself, which is your constitutional right, the author and the publisher assume no responsibility for your actions.

Any people depicted in stock imagery provided by Thinkstock are models, and such images are being used for illustrative purposes only. Certain stock imagery © Thinkstock.

Print information available on the last page.

ISBN: 978-1-5043-8899-3 (sc)
ISBN: 978-1-5043-8900-6 (e)

Library of Congress Control Number: 2017960586

Balboa Press rev. date: 12/04/2017

Contents

Introduction

Why I wrote this book?

I needed a reset. After years of doing what I thought I wanted to do, what people thought I should be doing and what I believed I should be doing I started hitting brick wall after brick wall. I wasn't hitting brick walls due to a lack of knowledge or planning. I was hitting brick walls because everything I had believed or thought I had known to be true began to feel like a betrayal. I had done what I was **supposed** to do. Finished school, landed a great job, built family, had a house (it was never home) and seemed to be progressing at the same rate as everyone else I knew. But this is where the problems began. I started realizing nothing I had achieved on a personal professional level met my needs.

I was burnt out and thirsty as hell! I started searching. And before long I was completely engrossed in any and everything involving self-help. Many of the themes did not speak completely to my needs. I could not clearly draw connections between self-esteem issues and getting the life I wanted. My understanding of many of the self-help themes was rudimentary to say the least. I kept studying.

When I discussed self-help with my friends and family many expressed the same frustration; lack of understanding for the connectedness between self-help themes and personal growth and development. For these reasons, many people never seek help through the self-help industry. The more I learned, and began to apply the theories and ideals to my own life the more things seemed to change in my favor. The benefits of understanding and being able to apply self-help ideas to your life is immeasurable. The *Conspiracy of You* was born; to assist others in understanding that self-help is personal growth and not simply a way to believe that you are beautiful. Being beautiful is only the beginning.

The *Conspiracy of You* is a brick wall story. It is about how brick wall encounters can force us to become more self-aware which frees us to be whatever we chose. The book was birthed from the knowledge I obtained when trying to overcome my brick wall experiences. What are brick wall stories? Brick wall stories are stories about experiences in which the individual must run into a brick wall in their own understanding to be awakened to new ideas about old ways of being.

Exhausted from my own brick wall experiences I began studying everything I could get my hands on about how to change and create the life I wanted. In the *Conspiracy of You*, I will share with the reader how mindset changes and intentional living became the keys to the obtaining the personal freedom I was seeking. None of the change I was seeking came without provocation. Change rarely does. I had to learn that I was the common denominator in both my wins and losses. And that although I often thought I knew it all, none of what I knew was getting me what I wanted.

Through story I will share with the reader how I learned to find a balance between being arrogant and base. Doing so allowed me to be authentic. This authenticity was fertilizer for opportunities to develop that supported my intentions and assisted in the creation of the life I desired. I hope my use of transparent expression allows the reader to see clearly how increased self-awareness, a growth mindset and intentional living, makes the life we want available to us.

CHAPTER 1

Welcome to the Conspiracy of You

Traditional thinking defines conspiracy in terms of legality; conspiracy refers to an illegal secret plan to commit an unlawful act[1].

That is not what we are talking about here!

The Conspiracy of You is about a process of personal growth, intentional planning and seeming coincidences that conspire (work together) to assist in the creation of the life you desire. Simply put, *The Conspiracy of You* is, the manifestation of the plan for your life.

Changing your Mind. Enjoying the benefits of the conspiracy begins with a change in mindset. To achieve something different than what we have, we must do something different. This is not a new idea. What is new, is understanding how personal growth and the way we view ourselves determines our ability to achieve our goals as well as our ability to support others. To change our mindset, we must change the way we think about ourselves, our abilities, talents and experiences. We must consider who we are versus who we want to be. Change requires a growth mindset. The growth mindset is one that recognizes challenges as opportunities unlike the fixed mindset.

---

[1] http://www.dictionary.com/browse/conspiracy. April 17, 2017.

The growth mindset says keep going, work harder, we can do it. The growth mindset sees opportunities, understands the possibility of success or failure; however, chooses to go forward because the potential to expand is greater than the ease of stasis. A growth mindset knows failure is always possible but so too is success.

Feeling stuck and helpless, are symptoms of a fixed mindset. When we doubt ourselves, we are using a fixed mindset. The fixed mindset is unable to see solutions. For some, this way of thinking has developed because of life's conditioning; past hurts, failures, disappointments, lack of support and low self-esteem. A fixed mind believes, "I knew we couldn't do it." This supported doubt causes us to behave in ways that protect us from potential failures through limiting self-sabotage.

Listen to the fixed mind. Become aware of it. Listen to the growth mind. Become aware of it. Now choose to stay where you are (fixed) or become what you want (growth). This choice determines the mindset you must follow. To be fixed is to be static. Not changing. Reluctant. For some it is being stuck.

To grow is to be fluid, open and ready.

A growth mindset is a part of *The Conspiracy of You*. Growth does not eliminate doubt, and fear, however, it does erode it; for these reasons continued growth is necessary.

Living Intentional. The conspiracy thrives on clearly set intentions; the ability to manifest and realize your desires through action lies with clearly set intentions. Intentions are the plan. Intentions are goals or determinations to do something, or be something.

Productivity studies continue to identify goal setting as a primary key to success. Setting goals is one way of intentional living. Some suggest writing your goals down and sharing them with someone whose opinion you value. Life coaches and gurus will advise you to carry them around with you. Having a written plan serves as a physical reminder; the written plan is an accountability manager. Written plans can be a way to measure progress: As you reach a milestone you can mark it off the list. Having a physical representation of your successes can be motivational. When we are motived by our performance we are more likely to continue the work.

However, you choose to do so, you **must** set your intentions before the conspiracy can take off.

Intentions guide the conspiracy.

Acting as goals, clearly set intentions create success.

Intention setting[2]. To set clear intentions, you first need to remove any ideas of could have, would have, should have been, and start thinking about what you want now. Second, with a clear idea in mind of what you want, you must determine the process by which to achieve it. Step three requires a little leg work in the form of research. Forth, after you have identified the process by which to achieve your goal; whether it is therapy to overcome abuse and forgive those around you or college to earn a degree, set a reasonable timeline to achieve each step in the process to reach your goal. Now that you have identified what you want, researched the process, and set your intentions, you are ready for the conspiracy to take hold.

After you have set your intentions the Universe, those seeming coincidences: the conspiracy, goes to work supporting you. It is up to you to recognize the *Conspiracy of You*. The Universe supports intention

---

[2] Gary Zukav. Chapter 7: Intention I. The Seat of the Soul: 25th Anniversary Edition. Simon & Schuster. March 2014.

and action. Each person must do the work assigned to the process by which they have identified to reach their goals.

Our intention creates our reality. -Dr Wayne Dyer

The Conspiracy of You is Manifest Destiny for the soul. Manifest Destiny[3], a 19th century doctrine that created a nation, was based on the belief of exceptionalism, divine right and a mission to expand. It was a narrative created to support the settlers desire for territorial expansion. The *Conspiracy of You* is the narrative we create to support our goals. Manifest Destiny was their plan. Here is ours: Set intentions, be clear, do the work, trust the process, live in grace. What you want develops from what you do. The life we want does not fall in our laps.

Whatever comes, comes through work! No matter how big the *Conspiracy of You* becomes, it will never manifest without the work. The divine right to have the life we want lies in our willingness to do what is necessary to achieve our goals. We have the divine right to pursue, build, and have anything we are willing to earn. We are each exceptional, possessing unique talent compatible with those of others yet specific to us. While it is not a how-to, this book presents an opportunity for us to consider how we are both responsible for creating and deserving of the lives we desire.

---

[3] https://en.wikipedia.org/wiki/Manifest_destiny. Accessed June 2016.

CHAPTER 2

Recognizing the Conspiracy

To recognize the conspiracy, you must pay attention to the small things turning in your favor. This is the Universe working on your behalf. These things will not always feel favored for example the sudden unexpected ending of a friendship. Sometimes the change we want requires a complete demolition and rebuild of our lives including the ending of some relationships. You will know it is the conspiracy because amid the demolition a new foundation will be poured. This foundation will consist of opportunities, support and people coming into your life that are there to help you build this new thing. Those unexplained confusing losses and gains are your conspiracy! Pay attention. Remember the changes are in support of your goals.

New opportunities will eventually become welcoming rather than intimidating; that's your conspiracy!

You will recognize the conspiracy by the changes in your personal environment (friends, opportunities, location, personal connections). There is a reason for this. Those intense connections you felt may not serve your new goals. Do not blame those around nor hold grudges. The Universe is assisting with your plans by reordering your priorities. You may start to feel out of place everywhere because you are not quite ready for the new thing however you are past that old thing. I compare it to Freshmen year feelings. By the time each of us reaches Freshman status in any area of life we are signifying growth beyond elementary level thinking; however, we are not quite ready to be Senior or expert. Therefore, being in those new circles can feel almost as weird as being in the old circles. The difference is, in the new circle you are learning and growing instead of teaching or staving off boredom.

You may be feeling disoriented by this feeling of being out of place. Disorientation is an important element of personal growth. It signifies change. Allow this feeling to manifest your desire to move forward. Disorientation can be painful; painful like physical growing pains.

You know the ones that come in the middle of the night while you are asleep causing your body to contort when all you want to do is rest. Some of us stumble out of bed trying to work the pain out. However, the pain subsides best through relaxation. The same is true of the disorientation associated with personal growth. Relax into who you are becoming.

Disorientation is an element of personal change. And the pains of personal growth can amount to the same level of pain as those physical growing pains. When you are growing, some nights are sleepless. Some nights require no sleep. Somedays your mind will seem to be clear; Some days it will feel as if it will never be clear again. These are the pains of growth. The only pain worse is the pain of never having pursued your dream because you never created a plan. Relaxing into the changes can lessen the pain. See the changes as moving you closer to your goals.

Disorientation is a correlate of change. It occurs when there is a disruption to your reference points; personal mental signals acting as guides, teaching us how to handle every situation in a way that preserves our being. Old reference points will not work in the new process. By setting intentions, deciding to do something different, be something different you are responsible for changing your reference points. Your perception must change.

If you currently see more hate, helplessness, hopelessness, boundaries and general negativity in life, to truly recognize the conspiracy, you will need to address these feelings. It starts with self-love. When you love, honor and respect yourself and show that same love to the world; the world reflects it back to you. This is a new season. A new mindset is required. You must let go of the old things and ways of being.

Disorientation is about resetting your perception, shaking away the old and making space for the new. When you relax into the process of disorientation, and begin to view the world as more supportive, it will become more supportive. Each person lives in the world they create for themselves. Disorientation is the beginning of a mental reset which supports the creation of the life we plan for. Accepting disorientation as a step in the process to creating the life you want is recognition of the conspiracy.

CHAPTER 3

Selfishness in the Conspiracy of You

This is not an asshole pass, to behave however you please in the name of achieving your dreams. Do not start strutting around like the new peacock on the yard. The conspiracy requires selfless selfishness. Our purposes are equally great. There is no room for disrespect nor disregard of others; to do so is disrespectful to yourself. There is no pushing anyone else down to get ahead.

Selfishness in the conspiracy of you is about self-motivation, putting your needs first and investing in yourself. COY selfishness is adding action to your plans; manifestation through action. Don't keep creating mantras, plans and new year's resolutions. Those things, on the surface, appear to be about being a part of the crowd. Being a part of the crowd is fine if, the crowd is going where you want to go. Instead create the thing/s specific to your dreams. Words will not get the work done, action will. What gets you moving? How do we get started?

Motivation. When I started writing this book, I knew I had to include a section on motivation. Motivation has been described as the reason or reasons for one's behaviors. Some individuals in the self-help community call it your 'why', the things that drives you to do what you do. I believed motivation was an external environmental factor therefore I began researching what motivates people expecting to find a list of things. There is tons of information and research on motivation and how to motivate this person or that person. Conversely, the only thing clear from all the research was, for it to be sustainable motivation must be intrinsic.

Intrinsic motivation[4] lives in you. It is based on the internal reward system. Intrinsic motivation is doing it for reasons that will not necessarily result in external rewards. The person who feeds the homeless without posting it to social media is likely operating on intrinsic motivation. This is the motivation that sustains success.

External motivational factors are limited in their effectiveness by time and space. Consider how quickly we fall back in to our old ways after that free personal training session at the gym is over. For me, as soon as the training sessions end, my drive to work out begins to dwindle. All over again, I find myself searching for something, anything to motivate me to get back into the gym. Although external motivational factors do not seem as effective as intrinsic motivation, they can work to support intrinsic motivating factors. The coach/athlete relationship is one instance in which external motivational factors support intrinsic motivation. Although the successful athlete usually has a healthy relationship with intrinsic motivation the motivation of a coach supports that success by guiding the athletes training. This motivation is relationship based. The trainer or coach supports the athlete's success however, absent intrinsic motivation the external motivation provide by a coach is fleeting.

In the *Conspiracy of You* it is important to find intrinsic motivation. It is the only motivation that will keep us going when all else fails. We must be doing whatever we are doing for reasons that no one else can control. If not, the moment those external factors change, the ability

---

[4] Motivating Your Intelligent But Unmotivated Teenagers. Dennis Bumgarner, ACSW, LCSW. http://behavior-coach.com/EbookMotivatingVer3.pdf.

to keep going will change. One way to think about this is, when you are fundamentally driven, whether you work from home or in your company's office your productivity will not change. You will work equally as hard from your kitchen table as you do in your cubicle.

And then there is the motivation that comes from reaping the benefits of your performance. Staying with the example of motivation for weight loss purposes. Seeing the number on the scale decrease because of your hard work is tantamount to having someone guide you through the process. That motivation is intrinsic! Be selfish in that way, seek the intrinsic motivation of doing the work. The practice of chasing motivation with results may not be popular but it works. Be selfish enough that you learn to do the work that motivates you to keep going. Resolutions, mantras, plans and the like can be beneficial if you understand that the motivation to achieve the desired goal lies in performance. Find what motivates you to keep moving toward your goals.

Self-Love/Putting Yourself first. We are all connected therefore loving yourself teaches you how to love others. Learning to love yourself includes lessons in learning to love and accept others. When you learn to appreciate, and accept yourself doing the same for others becomes easier.

The selfishness required for you to love and appreciate yourself is an incubator for you to do the same for others. Go to the spa, steal a few moments alone to read, take a bike ride through your neighborhood or whatever you do to free your mind and you will not feel judgmental of others who pamper themselves. The feeling you get when you take care of yourself are the same feelings others get when they do the same. Service to others is important; contrarily, putting aside our own needs to meet those of another can be an ego trip. Therefore, be careful of selfish motivations to serve others.

The capacity to be of service to others places us in a position of strength. It feeds the ego's need to be appear strong. When living in the conspiracy we are required to check the ego. Let someone be of service to us. We must learn to love ourselves enough to understand our worthiness to be supported.

Learning to love yourself and put you first, is a lesson in vulnerability. Allowing others to be of service to you shows your willingness to participate in life on the same terms as others. To be vulnerable is to be open to new opportunities, possibilities and experiences that may not always be favorable; however, knowledge of those experiences is valuable. They teach us more about who we are; Putting us in tune with our strengthens, weaknesses, likes and dislikes. In times of vulnerability, we are most receptive to those opportunities in life that can take us from mediocrity to extraordinary.

Still the conspiracy is for everyone. Therefore, be careful in your judgement of others. Appreciate their freedom to be themselves. Appreciation of others is precipitated by appreciation of self.

The conspiracy for your life does not diminish others. The conspiracy of you requires you to honor yourself and others. The conspiracy of you is the conspiracy for all. Self-care is a prerequisite to all other care. If you cannot feel for yourself, you certainly cannot feel for others. Lack of self-empathy leads to irrational emotional reliance and expectations of others. It makes everything feel pointless. "Why should I feel for them? No one felt for me" can be the message playing in your mind when you are not in tuned to you. This can lead to disregard and disrespect of self and others. No matter what focus on you. Get you well.

There is a reason why every emergency readiness plan requires the individual to secure themselves before attempting to help anyone else. On a plane, you are advised to secure your oxygen mask first, even parents, secure your mask first in the event of loss of oxygen in the cabin. If you cannot swim do not attempt to save your drowning friend, you will both parish. Get help. This is the logic I am asking you to apply in the Conspiracy of You. Take care of you before attempting to take care of others.

Invest in Yourself. To invest in ourselves is to prepare an investment for our community. When we increase our skills and knowledge, we add to the community's social capital.

> *I want to grow. I want to be better. You grow. We all grow. We're made to grow. Either you evolve or you disappear. – Tupac Shakur*

CHAPTER 4

Grace in the Conspiracy of You

Grace is required in the conspiracy of you. Grace for yourself and others. Grace in the conspiracy of you prevents you from encroaching on and dismissing others. Grace is often defined as the extension of courteous goodwill. Another spiritually based definition says, grace is the free and unmerited favor of God. However, you chose to define it, grace is simply the recognition and acceptance of differences. Grace says, "I see you and it's all good." Grace says, "You irk but I irk too."

Grace is the pause a driver gives to a pedestrian who chooses to cross the street outside of the crosswalk. Grace is the warm smile the bank teller gives you when your day seems to be going all wrong. Grace is a whiff of your favorite scent out of nowhere when you seem to be surrounded by trash. Grace says I see you.

Grace is all around, all the time. We take it for granted, almost never giving reverence to it. Grace appears in those moments when things seem difficult. It presents itself in what can easily be considered mediocrity. Grace are those moments at the gas station when you really do not have money for all that you need and the person in front of you looks back and says, "I am paying for her stuff too." Grace is not something for which we can ever be worthy of through our own actions. It is a courtesy.

Grace can make you stop to say thank you when saying thank you is the furthest thing from your mind. Grace is the right on time call from your parents to help when they didn't know you needed it. It happens to all of us. Through learning to participate in the conspiracy for our lives, we begin noticing and receiving more grace. It's sufficient.

Grace is free to everyone. Grace is an ego balancer. It removes the need for us to be egotistical. It makes the victim card less appealing. Grace eliminates the need for blame. Grace allows us to be well through difficult times. It asks us to focus on what we do have instead of what we believe is missing, never requiring us to become content with less; in its place patience.

Grace asks us to love others as we love ourselves. See for them what we want for ourselves.

Through grace we learn, nothing is owed but everything is valued. Grace can move you from anger to forgiveness. Since grace is the courteous extension of goodwill we must forgive to truly realize the beauty of grace. It's unending. Even when you hate them for the moment grace solicits one's change of mind to love instead.

It is a choice to view life this way. It is a choice to believe that things happen for us and not to us. Everything bares a lesson.

Every hard time is swathe in grace. It is the protection we do not always feel; however, it is always there. Grace allows us to experience hard things without devastation. Grace carries us through brokenness. When our lives are in disarray yet things keep happening to carry us along, that is grace. That is God saying I see you.

It is not earned. It is not for sale. It is given. Therefore, it is required that we give it freely. Even to those we do not deem worthy. Grace is not about worthiness. It is about humanness. The *Conspiracy of You* can be an ego boosting monster truck, climbing over and destroying everyone in its wake if we do not allow the grace extended to us, to become an extension of us.

On our path, as we meet things and people that do not seem in line with our goals, extend them the courteous goodwill of following their own path whether it furthers ours or not. This is grace in *The Conspiracy of You*. Freeing others to support or not, follow or not, with no change to the status quo of the relationship, is all grace.

CHAPTER 5

Fear in the Conspiracy of You

Fear will allow us to walk away from our destiny. Do not submit to it! Fear will keep us stranded in jobs or relationships that are killing our souls. Don't let it. Instead allow the fear to inspire you. It is a signal that perhaps you are on the right path.

Change is scary because it's new. It's like the curve on an unfamiliar road, a little unnerving because we don't know what's on the other side but proceeding is necessary if we want to stay on the road. When we make the personal adjustments, there will be fear in the success of those changes.

Even when you are winning, there is fear! There is the fear that no matter how great this feels, no matter how much you want it, taking a chance on it could result in failure.

Coming to terms with the decision to follow our path and to become whatever we want, will be scary. However, it is not scarier than not taking a chance.

I promise you, following your dream will be scary.

There is fear of the potential to fail.

Allow the fear and the disorientation it brings to be your ammunition. Fear can propel us into action. The fear of staying in place must become greater than the fear of moving forward if, fear is to be motivation; let it.

Two quick reminders that it is time to move on.

1. Feeling like your spirit is dying where you are, or

2. Feeling like the life is being choked out of you when no one has their hands around your throat.

Fear can be sweaty heart pounding anxiety.

Fear tried to stop me from pursuing my purpose. I used to wake up at the crack of dawn to go to work. For years, I allowed myself to believe that I was doing this to achieve some arbitrary corporate career goal that I had set for myself. The truth is, I went in super early because I hated the place, and wanted to get out of there as soon as possible EVERYDAY. My philosophy became, "in early, out early". I was cheating myself and the employer out of my best. I eventually left the company. The soul sickening pain was too much. The safety net it created was beginning to choke me. The fear of any potential financial loss became less fearful than the reality that I was losing myself! I was in the middle of disorientation.

Fear is a part of disorientation, therefore a part of the conspiracy. Learning to live in the conspiracy requires us to use fear as a reminder that we sometimes need to move on from a situation that no longer serves us.

Fear was asking me to love me enough to lessen the pain in favor of being who I was.

It asks each of us the same question. Then it challenges us to take a chance on ourselves. It challenges us to stop putting our dreams off.

I took the leap. I left my safety net. Some days were scary as hell, but others were so awesome that I would forget the scary ones. I left the corporate setting to support my family, help my husband build our business.

And it was scary. Winning is scary. The fear in winning is that no matter how great this all seems, it can go away today. However, after you take the initial big leap, you now have an outline of what leaping looks like so, the fear will be recognizable in the future. Take the leap. Get the roadmap.

Fear is good. Understand it as a step in the process of achieving the life you want.

CHAPTER 6

The Stall & Reorientation

And sometimes when we think have made it over the humps in life, everything gets creepily quiet and our next move becomes more unclear than our last so we stall.

Stall (n): a place; (v): state of being stopped, stopped due to overload

Decide which stall is yours. Are you in a holding place or are stopped due to overload? Both conditions are perfect for refining our development. The type of stall determines the plan of action. In both instances, we must move through the stall to realize the dream, the life, the love we want. Mental overload can signal the need to clear our plate: Declutter thinking and adjust our mindset.

Whether it is physical or mental, stalls are holding places. Be still. Your incubator is safe. The stall is the place where we learn to marry new ideals with those of the world we feel we've left behind. This will not be without discord; things do not change in concert. Reorientation, the stall is the final exam; quizzing us how to live NOW, with new information in a world that perhaps no longer seems to fit us.

Everything you need to be successful is always developing right on time for you. The holding place is signaling a need to slow down. Look around, see where you are compared to where you want to be.

We all stall. The stall signifies the last lap of the race. There will be other races but for now finish this one.

The stall can be a self-check point or a disaster. Pay attention. Don't let the responsibility of a cleaned-up act limit you. The stall is the final walk thru. The opportunity to get over pettiness, to accept your responsibility to grow up and grow others. The stall is the tool kit tester.

It challenges a lesson's applicability as well as our determination to be better every day. It's not a comparison of others, you versus them. You can only be a better version of yourself.

The stall is where you wait. Growth requires patience. There is a feeling of being stuck or stalled. In those moments of stall, reorientation, the act of changing focus or direction, is beginning.

Reorientation requires us to utilize our new perspective to view relationships that may or may not have changed in concert with your new direction. Of course, you have changed but what about the things and people around you? Rarely will you find yourself on the exact same path, in the exact same place, at the same time as anyone else in your life. This is the time for you to increase your reach and use grace. Connect with persons in seemingly similar places as you; those who are a little further along on their journey would be best. This will help with the difficulty of reorientation because perhaps they can share with you the normalcy of the fear, doubt and anxiety associated with change.

Now grace, use grace in dealing with those who have not reached your level of growth. Remember, you were once where they are. Do not turn away from them, instead, love them graciously. Loving graciously means, loving without judgement however, with support.

There will be moments filled with glimpses of your past that will remind you why you chose to move on. The old things no longer fit. There will always be these times. They serve as forward reminders.

One night during a stall, I decided to go out with my girlfriends to celebrate someone's birthday. Although it had been years since I had blessed a club scene not much had changed; the dresses were still short; the ratio of men to women remained off balance; unrealistic expectations permeated the air but this time with every passing glance, my discomfort with being there grew. I was grossly aware of the reasoning. I no longer belonged. If for no other reason than, these were not my people. This was not my place.

There was nothing about the place or the people that caused my discomfort. My discomfort was a me thing. I had changed. The reasons I had previously enjoyed were no longer a factor in my life. The lonely need to belong was gone. In those moments, I realized I was completely comfortable in my own skin. This was during my stall; a final lesson about why the change I was working hard for was worth it, I had out grown my old needs.

The club scene did not change. My need to be there did. The reasons it felt good in the past were, in the past. I had developed a sense of self-worth that was far greater than any external being could affect. I did not need that club experience to realize my change. The experience worked to solidify what I was beginning to feel; secure in my self-worth, absent the need for external gratification.

Your new perspective will change your interactions with old inducements.

Your new self-care, self-love mindset will change everything. There will be moments when you want to rely on the old way of procrastination and stagnation; however, this new mindset will not allow it. I am not sure certain why this happens during the stall except, *in my personal experience, it became more difficult to disregard my goals after I realized the success of everything I attempted rested on my ability to just do it.* I have reached the stalling position at least a hundred times in my life. Often, I lost the race in the stall because I never felt the worthiness necessary to succeed, to push through the last bits of bullshit.

In the stall, you must decide whether to go forward or turn back. Those are the only two options because by this time you have learned too much to remain stalled. You cannot stay, you must either run the race or go home. Others are waiting for their turn to be great so you must make a choice. Those that come behind you do not want to hear your story if you do not join the race. No one wants to hear the story of what you learned, if you stay in the stall.

The stall is not about boasting of your growth. It is about bursting out the gates ready to win and learn. The stall is the locker room before the game, the stall is the classroom, the stall is divorce, the stall is marriage, the stall is the introduction, your coach is in your head guiding you, your teammates are ready but it is upon you to make your entrance. Leave the stall. Success in the conspiracy requires you to leave the stall. You are worth it. The world is waiting on your goodness.

The stall.

CHAPTER 7

Living in the Conspiracy

Now that you've learned to recognize the conspiracy of you, let's talk about how you live in the conspiracy. Disclaimer:

*The conspiracy of you makes you feel like you rock and you do; therefore, you will need to check your ego, **A LOT.** Check it to make sure it's not in over drive. Make sure your determined success does not maliciously intentionally impede the success of others. The conspiracy of you is about them too!*

When learning to live the COY it is essential that we understand the relationship between the ego, humbleness and grace. The ego is the workhorse. The ego grinds. Its job is to make sure you reach those goals, that you win, at all costs. The ego does not have a heart therefore, the ego will ruin relationships if it means delivering a win. The ego does not care about relationships, spirit or love. The ego wants the success you have planned for. The ego does not give reverence to others, it just goes and goes until it reaches success. It never realizes the bridges it's burned or the minefield it created around you due to its drive to win. It only wants the trophy. It takes its role seriously.

The reckless fervor with which the ego works must be checked. Finding the balance between getting what you want and respecting others is principal to the process; Continued success and happiness depend on it. This balance is achieved through grace and humbleness, i.e. your heart. Grace, the courtesy extension of goodwill to others allows us to be ourselves, work on our process and not disrespect others as they attempt to do the same. Grace means understanding a denied invitation is not always a denial of support. Grace means understanding that as much as we want for our lives, others want the same for theirs. Sometimes those desires will not line up and that is okay. Grace simply says, next time friend!

Grace teaches us to be humble. Humble in our success because we know what the behind the scenes of success looks like with paperwork scattered about and multiple search engines going all at once. This teaches us to respect the hard work required for the success of others. We must be humble in knowing, although our thing did not make it, does not mean we cannot celebrate someone else success. One success makes way for another. Seeing success lets us know success is possible. We should all look for it and celebrate it where ever you may find it. The humbleness and grace we share is heart.

Reluctant companions they are, the ego and the heart work best when coupled. The ego is important, it gets the work done. The heart holds us accountable. It is our responsibility to make sure they respect each other.

Taking the leap, making the decision to live the conspiracy of you is scary, without the fear of the fall, the leap would not be as great. There is something about the possibility of falling on your face that makes the temptation to leap even greater. Every seeker comes to a place in life where the value of failure is as great as that of success. For without failure there is no success: every failure brings one closer to success.

Every moment I avoided or disregarded my goals, was followed by days filled with coercive coincidences encouraging me to make up what I missed and push past where I would have been. For me the chance that I may fail became less scary than the security of not moving forward so I jumped.

And the fear of falling face first encourages us to work hard so we prevent the face fall. In these moments of fear, allow fear to become a friend. A constant companion to the desire to succeed. Leading us to search for it in our dreams, fear plays hide and seek. Leading us to believe we have overcome it only to run smack into it with our guards down. When we are awake, we expect to meet it somewhere between completing our daily task and turning off the lights for the night. With this truth, you prepare to take leaps, change your mind, be who you want to be, with fear pressing itself into your back. Know that without its presence there would be no alarm signaling the perfect time to jump.

The perfect time is when the struggle to stay becomes more herculean than the pain of a potential fall. The perfect time to jump is when there is less space under your feet than there is on the landing pad. The perfect time to jump is when your anxiety seems to be holding you tighter than ever. Jump, free yourself from the pressure to be what you've always been. Be what you want to be; Do what you want to do. Follow the conspiracy.

The conspiracy calls you out of obscurity. Listen to it.

Living in the conspiracy is about learning to take chances on yourself. It's about learning to believe in your ability to do or be whatever it is you are willing to work hard to become. Living in the conspiracy of you is learning to create comfort wherever you want to be instead of staying in the comfort of a limited life/potential.

Living in the conspiracy does not mean fear will disappear. However, you will learn to recognize fear as opportunity and push past it. In this way, you will begin to create new opportunities and eliminate limiting boundaries.

Creating Comfort in Uncomfortable Places. *Kindergarten was awesome, it's where I learned all my best stuff. My favorite part of each day was at the end when we gathered around Mrs. Mary for story time. Mrs. Mary was beautiful. Her tone was always calm and nonjudgmental; important for kindergarteners. During story time Mrs. Mary had this cool rocking chair which sat on top of a colorful braided rug in the middle of the classroom library. That library was magical. When we were in the library on the rug Mrs. Mary owned the classroom. It was the only time of day that the whole class paid attention without direction. Her sitting in the rocking chair in the library was direction enough.*

I am not certain which element of story time is responsible for it, but, there was a bond created between teacher and students which allowed a room of rowdy, whinny five-year old's, to become receptive to the experience of kindergarten. Mrs. Mary used things like books, colors, stuffed animal and her story telling to create comfort for us in what was initially an uncomfortable place.

When you learn to live fully in the conspiracy of you, you will be able to create comfort in your life in those uncomfortable times of change and decision making. The ability to create comfort in those times of discomfort, helps us to overcome limiting fears. When we can overcome our fears, we open ourselves to the ability to create the life we want. While becoming less discourage by fear, we become more willing to invest time, energy and resources into efforts that further our purpose.

Get a rainbow rug or a whatever is needed to make the journey to the life you want comfortable in the most uncomfortable times.

When I need comfort, I lay flat on my back in complete silence. This allows me to let all the chaos I am feeling around me continue as it needs to, while I reenergize. Doing this, lying flat on my back alone, in silence gives me a euphoric feeling of being absent and present. Because while I am zoned out I am still completely in the process.

Comfort is created based on individual needs; what works for me may not work for you. The ability to do so if invaluable to living in the conspiracy because as you continue to expand, you will find yourself consistently on the outside of your comfort zone. The desire to stretch will always be pulling. Sometimes harder than others.

Living in the *Conspiracy* requires an understanding of timing. There is a lot of work to be done before success can be fully realized. Still, the work does not stop after the career or life expansion you have been expecting happens. Every day we must create a plan for the day's success, an actionable plan which allows us to nurture our current successes while building new ones. Success and living the life you want does not simply happen. You cannot do the work once and expect the successes to continue. One win is an anomaly, multiple continued wins equals success. Find your Conspiracy and work it until you have the life you want.

In Conclusion

The *Conspiracy of You* is about personal growth and how life opens when we participate through intentional living in the development of the life we want. To tap into this level of personal growth the individual must be or seek to become more self-aware, exhibiting the ability to see oneself as separate and a part of the environment; conscious of personal strengthens, opportunities and desires. Separate from the environment in that we are individuals with character traits, abilities and feelings specific to us but not different than those of our peers. A part of the environment in that, if we grow our environment grows.

The *Conspiracy* encourages increased self-awareness through its insistence of the individual to pursue the life they want. By doing the work to change behaviors, mindset and environment to one conducive to success, we are challenged to become more self-aware.

Self-awareness, the ability to be introspective, is a super power that everyone can have. By learning to recognize and live the conspiracy of you, your self-awareness increases. Increased self-awareness has an innate ability to change one's quality of life through improved decision making. When we are aware of our strengths, opportunities, needs and desires we are better able to choose careers, lifestyles and relationships that suit us.

Self-awareness is empowering. Power is in the knowing. Knowing how valuable you are, understanding strengthens as gifts to be shared can encourage you to step into your dreams. We become empowered by learning to value and nurture strengthens while intentionally working on challenges. Self-awareness gives us the control to create whatever we want. The powerful awareness derived from the ability to cultivate your desires/dreams/life you want can be intoxicating. Take care with this awareness; you are responsible for how you use it.

The distinction of increased self-awareness is not binary; neither good nor bad, just different.

Through increased self-awareness, we extend grace to others because there is no expectation of perfection. When we become more self-aware, we learn to replace self-criticism and that of others with support. Learn better, do better, be better.

Increased self-awareness can seem difficult. It has a domino effect. The adjustments, the improved self-awareness, effects everyone. It is shy. Self-conscious. It wonders whether everyone in the room thinks it's a joke or not because perhaps, suddenly, not really but that's how change feels to people, you don't curse people out when they offend you. Those feelings are indicative of the timeliness with which the improved awareness happened. Everyone will be impacted by your increased self-awareness. Increased self-awareness, encourages us to understand our needs and how to meet them. This understanding makes it easier for us to understand the needs of others.

Living in the *Conspiracy* teaches the individual to acceptance the difficulty that comes with the freedom to create what you want. The difficulty I am speaking of lies in the inevitability of strained relationships. The difficulty of accepting that not everyone wants what you want. The difficulty of accepting, there is no success in wanting more for others than they want for themselves. There is success in the ability to accept and support others in ways they desire. Sometimes doing so will feel out of alignment with your purpose. It's not. Living in the *Conspiracy* of you does not require us to force others into our conspiracy. Nor does it give us the authority to determine the W's of someone else's conspiracy.

When our lives change, the lives of everyone around us are changed. The change is natural. The change occurs due to your changed responses to old questions which in turn creates new questions and responses.

Be gracious.

We may feel as if we have won the personal lottery while, those around us could be feeling a loss. A loss of the person they knew. Increased self-awareness leads us to be gracious with those who find our growth hard to swallow. This new way of being is ours not theirs. However, through our new awareness others can grow.

It is your responsibility to show others the value in growth. The last thing you want to do with your new awareness is to cause others to feel less than. If you go through a major life change and come out of it an asshole, it does not matter how successful you become, no one will respect or want your change. Most people do not want to be an asshole. They kind of stink! Be careful to ensure that the value of your new awareness can be realized through your living. Start doing more and saying less. Show your growth, do not just talk about it.

Kadosh – separate, transcend, distinction

The awareness of your ability to create the life you want doesn't automate that life. You must be present. You must be willing. You must do the work. You must be gracious.

Final Thoughts

When I started writing this book I thought I was sharing the gift of how to live the life you want with others. And I believe that information can be found here; however, this book was for me. Although sometimes I'd like to think of myself as a teacher, I know I will always be a student. I have lived the struggle to finding my own happiness; I had to learn to follow my own greatness, learning to believe in myself for real, and being at peace with the opportunities and challenges my journey offers. On my journey, I learned we all have a journey; we all have greatness to reach, opportunities to behold and challenges to overcome.

So how do we get to the map for our lives?

Take the first step; Press go. Start the journey and the map will reveal itself. Learning to recognize and participate in the conspiracy of you is the first step. There are things in this life that you are meant to do and if you let it, the Universe will get you to those things. You do the work.

While procrastinating completing writing the manuscript for this book I got caught up learning about quantum physics. Interest in the theory leaped into my consciousness absent my consent. Before this fascination began I was about as familiar with the theory of quantum physics as anybody else. Nothing I did to avoid writing seemed to replace my thoughts about quantum physics. Initially, I tried pushing the idea out of mind. I had no space for it. But a lot of ideas happen to me in this way so I had to consider what it meant. I started Googling. Then I bombarded by teenager with requests for clarity relating to the information I found on the google.

Trying to process this newly acquired knowledge left me restless for weeks. As soon as my head would hit the pillow a looped sound track of, 'all the little things, we can't see, that make up the big things we can see, all the little things we can't see that make up the big things we can see', would begin to play in my head. Even with those words playing in my head I continued to wonder what quantum physics had to do with anything.

Puzzled by the relationship my procrastination was developing with researching quantum physics I decided to write about it. It was only after I completed writing for day that I realized what I'd written. I had not shared those thoughts with anyone. I was embarrassed that I didn't know how to handle it. Here's what I wrote:

> *Quantum physics is all the little things we can't see that make up the big things we can see. Not the elephant in the room instead, the whole room. The whole idea of the Conspiracy of You is based on how the little things make up the big things and when you recognize this truth, the Universe rises to meet you.*

I was experiencing the *Conspiracy of You* in action, amid my efforts to complete this book. I wanted this book to happen. I did the work to make sure it happened. I fought through fear. I understood what it meant to my process. Now I was stalling. Quantum physics was my reminder. I had to finishing this book. It was a part of my conspiracy. I had to live it despite the fear and anxiety of its success or failure. I had to make sure that the reader understood completely, the Conspiracy of you does include God.

I needed quantum physics because I am a thinker. I needed to see God in this thing intellectually. The self-love, the love we share with others, quantum physics. Love is a small thing. But through love all things flow. God is love. He is everything. In everything. I could not finish this book without giving reverence to his omni essence. He is all.

He is all the little things we think he is too big to be and all the big things we think too small for Him. The wind that carries pollen from blossom to blossom. He is the sky that stays in place without need for our command. He is the nose of the plane piercing the sky with the sun and moon at just the right moment each day and night. The clouds that cover us and then showers the land. He is every star.

He is a whisper. A tear. The pain of labor and the joy of birth. Every beginning and ending.

He

is

not

magic.

Much greater instead. Magic is an illusion. He is not.

He is not the elephant in the room; He is the room. He is the lesson in the pain. Forgiveness.

He is.......

Therefore, only through recognition of God can your conspiracy truly be unlocked.

The deal with my quantum physics soundtrack was, I had been trying to finish this book without talking about God. I wanted to present a theory about getting what you want through increased self-awareness without talking about God. I had mulled the idea over in my head at least a million times and had decided that this book would be fine without explicitly mentioning God. It could not happen that way so God gave me quantum physics.

If He wasn't in it, it just couldn't be.

References

1 http://www.dictionary.com/browse/conspiracy. April 17, 2017.
2 Gary Zukav. Chapter 7: Intention I. The Seat of the Soul: 25th Anniversary Edition. Simon & Schuster. March 2014.
3 https://en.wikipedia.org/wiki/Manifest_destiny. Accessed June 2016.
4 Motivating Your Intelligent But Unmotivated Teenagers. Dennis Bumgarner, ACSW, LCSW. http://behavior-coach.com/EbookMotivatingVer3.pdf.

www.ingramcontent.com/pod-product-compliance
Lightning Source LLC
Chambersburg PA
CBHW030544290526
45786CB00004B/1861